A prese[nt]
visit to the Battle
of Britain Memorial
flight 2002

Love from
Katharine et.al.

WINSTON CHURCHILL

Quotations

JARROLD
PUBLISHING

CHURCHILL AT HIS DESK
ON HIS 8OTH BIRTHDAY
24 November, 1954

You ask, what is our aim? I can answer in one word:
Victory – victory at all costs, victory in spite of all terror,
victory, however long and hard the road may be;
without victory, there is no survival.

Courage is rightly esteemed the first of
human qualities because it is the quality
which guarantees all others.

THE MOST difficult things for a man to do are to
climb a wall leaning towards you, to kiss a girl leaning away
from you, and to make an after-dinner speech.

An appeaser is one
who feeds a crocodile
hoping it will
eat him last.

History will be kind to
me for I intend to
write it.

IT IS NO use saying 'we are
doing our best'. You have
got to succeed in doing
what is necessary.

CHURCHILL, ROOSEVELT AND STALIN AT THE YALTA CONFERENCE
February 1945

WINSTON CHURCHILL AS BOER WAR CORRESPONDENT IN
1900, Mortimer Menpes

No one can guarantee success
in war, but only deserve it.

Go into the sunshine and be happy with what you see.

IT WOULD be a great reform
in politics if wisdom could be made to
spread as easily and as rapidly as folly.

Man will occasionally stumble over the truth, but most of the time he will pick himself up and continue on.

I have never accepted what many people have kindly said, namely that I inspired the nation. Their will was resolute and remorseless, and as it proved, unconquerable. It was the nation and the race dwelling all round the globe that had the lion's heart. I had the luck to be called upon to give the roar!

WORLD WAR II VE DAY
8 May 1945

LET US LEARN our lessons.
Never, never, never believe any war will be smooth and easy...
Always remember, however sure you are that you
can easily win, that there would not be a war if
the other man did not think he also had a chance.

"LET US GO FORWARD TOGETHER"

If we open a quarrel between the past and present,
we shall find that we have lost the future.

Dictators ride to and fro upon
tigers which they dare not
dismount. And the tigers are
getting hungry.

I MUST POINT out that my rule of life prescribes as an
absolutely sacred rite smoking cigars and also the drinking of
alcohol before, after, and if the need be during all meals and in
the intervals between them.

MORALE-BOOSTING POSTER
FROM WORLD WAR II

The dead bird does not leave the nest.
(Said by an aging Winston Churchill when told that his fly was open.)

We are all worms.
But I do believe that I
am a glow-worm.

WE SHAPE our buildings;
thereafter they shape us.

CHURCHILL, BRITISH STATESMAN AND AUTHOR
Undated photograph

ROOSEVELT AND CHURCHILL AT THE CASABLANCA CONFERENCE
January 1943

The whole history of the world is summed up in the fact that, when nations are strong, they are not always just, and when they wish to be just, they are no longer strong.

So long as I am acting from duty and conviction, I am indifferent to taunts and jeers. I think they will probably do me more good than harm.

WITHOUT MEASURELESS and perpetual uncertainty the drama of human life would be destroyed.

I found that I could add
nearly two hours to my
working day by going to
bed for an hour after
luncheon.

A fanatic is one
who can't change
his mind and won't
change the subject.

IN WAR: *resolution*.
In defeat: *defiance*.
In victory: *magnanimity*.
In peace: *goodwill*.

WORLD WAR II VE DAY
8 May 1945

CHURCHILL LEAVING THE WHITE HOUSE
January 1952

When I was younger, I made it a rule
never to take strong drink before lunch.
It is now my rule never to do so before breakfast.

When you feel you cannot continue
in your position for another
minute, and all that is in human power has
been done, that is the moment when the
enemy is most exhausted, and when one
step forward will give you the fruits of the
struggle you have borne.

I HAVE TAKEN more out of
alcohol than alcohol has
taken out of me.

Solitary trees, if they grow at all, grow strong.

All wisdom is not new wisdom.

I AM PREPARED to meet my Maker.
     Whether my Maker is prepared for the great ordeal of meeting me is another matter.

WINSTON CHURCHILL, ILLUSTRATION IN
VANTIY FAIR, 1900

CHURCHILL AT HIS EASEL
Undated

When I get to heaven I mean to spend a considerable portion of my first million years in painting, and so get to the bottom of the subject.

Broadly speaking, human beings may be divided into three classes: those who are billed to death, those who are worried to death and those who are bored to death.

EVERYBODY HAS the right to pronounce foreign names as he chooses.

Personally I'm always ready to learn, although I do not always like being taught.

Where does a family start? It starts with a young man falling in love with a girl. No superior alternative has yet been found.

THERE IS no finer investment for any community than putting milk into babies.

**CHURCHILL, WIFE AND DAUGHTER AT
CHARTWELL MANOR, WESTERHAM, 1925**

The gratitude of every home in our island, in our Empire, and indeed throughout the world, except in the abodes of the guilty, goes out to the British airmen who, undaunted by odds, unwearied in their constant challenge and mortal danger, are turning the tide of the world war by their prowess and by their devotion. Never in the field of human conflict was so much owed by so many to so few.

*T*his is not the end, it is not
even the beginning of the end.
But it is, perhaps, the end
of the beginning.

GOLF IS AN ineffectual attempt to direct an
uncontrollable sphere into an inaccessible hole
with instruments ill-adapted to the purpose.

WINSTON CHURCHILL IN RAF UNIFORM,
1948

I know of no case where a man added
to his dignity by standing on it.

History with its flickering lamp stumbles along the trail of the
past, trying to reconstruct its scenes, to revive its echoes, and
kindle with pale gleams the passion of former days.

AT EVERY crisis the Kaiser
crumpled. In defeat, he fled;
in revolution, he abdicated; in
exile, he remarried.

WITH EISENHOWER, VE DAY,
8 May 1945

ENGROSSED IN HIS HOBBY
OF OIL PAINTING AT MIAMI BEACH

Writing a book is an adventure. To begin with it is a toy and an amusement. then it becomes a mistress, then it becomes a master, then it becomes a tyrant. The last phase is that just as you are about to be reconciled to your servitude, you kill the monster, and fling him about to the public.

It has been said that Democracy is the worst form
of government except all those other forms that
have been tried from time to time.

IN WARTIME...truth is so precious
that she should always be attended
by a bodyguard of lies.

A prisoner of war is a man who
tries to kill you and fails, and then
asks you not to kill him.

*I*t is a good thing for an uneducated man to read books of
quotations...The quotations when engraved upon the
memory give you good thoughts. They also make you
anxious to read the authors and look for more.

PERHAPS IT is better to
be irresponsible and right than to
be responsible and wrong.

*S*ay what you have to say and
the first time you come to a
sentence with a grammatical
ending – sit down.

CHURCHILL IN SOUTH AFRICA
1900

WINSTON CHURCHILL, ILLUSTRATION IN
VANTIY FAIR, 1900

Let us therefore brace ourselves to our duties, and so bear ourselves that, if the British Empire and its Commonwealth last for a thousand years, men will still say: 'This was their finest hour.'

Odd things animals.
All dogs look up to you. All cats
look down to you.
Only a pig looks at you as an equal.

I CANNOT PRETEND to feel impartial about colours.
I rejoice with the brilliant ones and am genuinely
sorry for the poor brown.

Secrecy is not to be measured in
altitude. If it were so, many might
think that 'Bottom Secret' would
be more forceful and suggestive.

WINSTON CHURCHILL INSPECTS THE
PARLIAMENTARY HOME GUARD, MAY 1942

Politics are almost as exciting as war, and quite as dangerous. In war you can only be killed once, but in politics many times.

Evils can be created much quicker than they can be cured.

IT IS A MISTAKE to look too far ahead. Only one link in the chain of destiny can be handled at a time.

There is nothing more exhilarating than to be shot at without result.

Continental people have sex life;
the English have hot-water bottles.

Too often the strong, silent man is silent only because
he does not know what to say, and is reputed strong
only because he has remained silent.

SAVING IS A very fine thing. Especially
when your parents have done it for you.

Everyone has his day and some
days last longer than others.

THE NEW FIRST LORD OF THE ADMIRALTY,
ARRIVING AT THE ADMIRALTY IN LONDON,
17 September 1939

My life is over,
but it is not yet ended.

*I*t is a socialist idea that making profits is a vice;
I consider the real vice is making losses.

Experts should be
on tap but never on top.

**CHURCHILL FLASHES HIS FAMILIAR
'V' FOR VICTORY SIGN**

Also in this series
William Shakespeare Quotations

First published in Great Britain in 1997 by
Jarrold Publishing Ltd
Whitefriars, Norwich NR3 1TR

Developed and produced by
The Bridgewater Book Company

Researched and edited by David Norley
Picture research by Vanessa Fletcher
Printed and bound in Belgium 2/01
Copyright © 1997 Jarrold Publishing Ltd
All rights reserved

ISBN 0-7117-0980-7

Acknowledgements

Jarrold Publishing would like to thank all those who kindly gave
permission to reproduce the words and visual material in this book;
copyright holders have been identified where possible and we
apologise for any inadvertent omissions.

We would particularly like to thank the following
for the use of pictures:
Corbis-Bettmann/Underwood, e.t. archive, Illustrated London News,
Mary Evans Picture Library, Rex features, UPI/Corbis-Bettmann.

Front and back cover: e.t. archive
Frontispiece: Rex Features
Endpapers: Illustrated London News

Quotations from the works of Sir Winston Churchill
© Sir Winston S. Churchill.

Produced in association with Curtis Brown on behalf of the
estate of Winston Churchill. Sources:

Great Contemporaries   *The River War*
History of the English-Speaking Peoples   *The World Crisis*
Lord Randolph Churchill   *The Second World War*
My Early Life   *Thoughts and Adventures*
The People's Rights   *While England Slept*